DON'T LOSE THE BALL
IN THE LIGHTS

And other life lessons from sports

Suzanne Detar

Wiser Today Publications, LLC
225 Seven Farms Dr., Suite 108,
Charleston, SC 29492
Copyright © 2018 Suzanne Detar
SuzanneDetar.com

ISBN-13: 978-1-946229-96-0
ISBN-10: 1-946229-96-2

Cover Design by Jan Marvin
Cover Photo by Lynn Cobb Photography

DEDICATION

To my children – Benjamin, Carly, and Jackson

TABLE OF CONTENTS

ACKNOWLEDGMENTS

My first debt of thanks goes to the people who inspired me to write the stories in this book.

Thanks and gratitude to the many athletes and coaches I value as teammates and instructors over the years— my little league baseball teammates and coaches with Elks 814, the neighborhood boys who always let me play, Pottstown Jr. and Sr. High School coaches and teammates, and my slow pitch softball pals. And thank you to the students and their parents, whom I've had the pleasure to coach over the years. Teaching adds a whole new level of learning and the thrill of seeing a student's improvement matches the thrill of scoring the triangle goal (see chapter 1).

Many stories in the book come from observing professional, Olympic, collegiate and youth athletes to whom I have no real personal connection, but who inspire many, including me. Thank you.

My biggest athletic influences come from my college

years at Lafayette College. Ann Gold, the field hockey and lacrosse coach during my tenure there, and the amazing group of women athletes who propelled both teams our senior year to top ten Division I national rankings and a trip to the Final Four in lacrosse. Collectively, they created an atmosphere of competition, growth, and appreciation for life beyond athletics and their influence is felt throughout this book.

The nearest and dearest athletic influences in this book are my kids, their friends and their teammates. They provided many of the insights that sparked the narratives on these pages. Ben, Carly and Jack – thank you for being who you are – with your passion, drive, kindness, support and wisdom – both on and off the athletic field and dance floor, and in and out of the pool.

Also, thank you to Sue Ellen Hawkins who got me to acknowledge that after more than 40 years of crafting and composing text, I can indeed call myself a writer. And thank you to my Tuesday evening Al-Anon Group – many of the Al-Anon principles subtly made their way into this book.

Thank you to my mentor, Steve Ferber. His insights and support are immeasurable.

I am grateful to the readers of *The Daniel Island News,* whose feedback to the original articles motivated me to continue writing and to turn those stories into this book.

To the wonderful staff at *The Daniel Island News* – thank you for covering for me when needed and for being supportive of this project.

Thank you to Lynn Cobb for her wonderful photography and a willingness to play along with my goofier photo requests.

Thanks to the Togami family, especially to Hannah, for agreeing to be the cover model and to pose for all the photos. She was a joy to work with…and a natural athlete.

Thank you to the Charleston RiverDogs for permission to use their ballpark to shoot the cover photo.

Thank you to Jan Marvin for the cover design. In addition to being an excellent graphic artist, her talents as an artist and her insight as a person are a blessing.

This book had several superb editors. The original articles were edited by Tom Ratzloff, a talented wordsmith and editor, and by Rosie Stieby, a passionate grammarian and eagle-eyed copyeditor. Thank you both for improving each article and correcting my mistakes.

And, an overwhelming thank you to a special editor and

friend - Elizabeth Bush. Beth took over my role as the editor of *The Daniel Island News* and she did the final edit of this book – I could not have trusted the paper or this book to a better writer, editor and person. Beth knows how to change a word or a punctuation mark to make a sentence sing, but more importantly, she knows how to make a person feel great. Thanks to Beth for improving my work beyond measure!

Thank you to the earliest influences in my life - Mom, Dad, Mike and Michele – I loved growing up with you and playing, following, and talking sports over the years. And I'm especially thankful that Mom and Dad provided athletic, educational, and life enhancing opportunities to us three kids. I miss you, Mom!

And, finally, thank you to my husband, Tom Werner, for his continual support. He has improved my writing by his edits and by helping me understand how to add humor to the mix - plus he makes life a lot of fun!

Thank you. Enjoy.

- INTRODUCTION -

FIELD SMARTS – DON'T LOSE THE BALL IN THE LIGHTS

I love sports. I love everything about sports. As a child and through my college years, I played, watched, imagined, developed, analyzed, ate, lived and breathed sports. But, somewhere along the road to adulthood, sports took on a smaller and smaller place in my life. As I morphed into a lawyer, mother, wife, writer, newspaper publisher and parent, less and less of my time became devoted to playing, strategizing and watching sports. Kind of a royal bummer, right?

And then, in the spring of 2008 I was at a four-day swim meet with my oldest son, Ben, which means I had a lot of free time sitting at the pool between events. I started reading a book entitled *A Life Worth Leading*, the Lutheran workbook version of Rick Warren's *A Purpose Driven Life*. There was an exercise that required me to write down the five most important gifts God has given me and the five things in my life that I've done that I feel the best about. Guess what? Sports items dominated both lists.

The purpose of making the lists was to help determine what a life worth leading would be like for me.

I then began brainstorming on ways to incorporate athletics back into my life and make life better for someone else. I came up with several promising ideas and immediately put one into action – writing a regular sports column. As the owner and editor of a weekly newspaper published on Daniel Island, SC, I had the outlet and resources to put my column into action. So in 2008, I launched a new sports column in my community newspaper, named it Field Smarts, and began writing about life lessons from sports.

My goal was to use the column as a way to make life better for someone else. At the time, I asked myself if this was arrogant – could a column I write really make life better for another person? That was a lofty goal. My hope was that those articles would not come across as preachy, but as lessons that would inspire, motivate, or lead someone in a direction that would make a difference.

To my surprise, the feedback I received from the column was amazing. Not only were people telling me that the column was changing their lives, but that they were sharing the column with their children and that it was the catalyst to conversation around the dinner table.

Field Smarts was honored that year by the South Carolina Press Association as the top sports column in the state for weekly newspapers.

So, just what is "field smarts?"

The phrase "field smarts," sometimes referred to as "game sense," is defined as a player's innate sense of where to be and how to play; knowing where to be at the right time; and great intuition on the field. Through analogy, the Field Smarts column parlayed sports lessons into life lessons.

Jump forward five years later to October 30, 2013. Two important things happened. First, it marked the tenth anniversary of the publication of the first edition of the newspaper I birthed in 2003. Second, it was the day that I told myself, through a self-fulfilling affirmation motivated by Jack Canfield of *Chicken Soup for the Soul* fame, "I enjoy being a New York Times best-selling author."

And hence, the actions necessary to turn that affirmation into reality began with earnest. It was time to turn Field Smarts into a book. After a few diversions along the way, the motivation came back and the book is complete

A little background information. Since the spring of 2001, and continuing each spring up until today, my newspaper and our island town gear up for the Family

Circle Cup (recently renamed the Volvo Car Open), a women's professional tennis event that brings 90,000 plus people and the top players in the world to our community for 10 days of amazing tennis. Each year at Family Circle Cup time, I am reminded of a morning in 2007. I didn't have very good "court smarts" that day as I competed against international journalists in the media tennis tournament that is held each year prior to the Family Circle semifinals on Saturday. Basically, we media types are a bunch of coffee-guzzling, sometimes less than fit journalists trying to compete in an event that showcases some of the most athletic talent in the world. We make a living critiquing the abilities of the players we cover, and we don't always do it in the most positive light.

When my partner, *The Daniel Island News* freelance photographer Doug Pinkerton, and I took to the court, I was feeling confident. Never mind that I had never competed in a tennis match in my life. I saw that the lady on the other side of the net, an AP photographer, was the basic journalist – older and much heavier than me. Plus she was wearing a knee brace. I was ready to sail through into the second round.

Wrong.

Besides being reminded that appearances can be deceptive, I got a lesson on the importance of placement, i.e. tennis game sense. It was like that AP photographer was a magnet that I kept hitting the ball to. And she never hit it to me or Doug. In fact, she had a light touch and always placed the ball somewhere on the court where we were not and where we couldn't make the play.

We were off the court pretty fast that morning, giving us plenty of time to prepare for covering the real event.

By analogy, life's field smarts are just that - making mistakes until we learn to do it right so we can be in the right place at the right time.

Of course, the most practical lesson I ever learned, I learned the hard way: don't lose the ball in the lights. And if you do, don't try and guess where it will come down. As a Little League centerfielder, I was the only girl in the league and thrilled to make the All-Star team. The All-Star game was the first time I ever played at night under the lights. With a runner on first and one out midway through the game, a high fly ball was hit to shallow centerfield. I rushed in to field it but lost it as it went above the lights. I never found it when it came back out from under the glare of the lights. I missed it. It hit me square in the chest! Red-faced and red-chested, I picked up the ball and threw the runner out at second base.

So what's the life lesson? Don't give up, even when you're embarrassed and in pain.

SUZANNE DETAR

- Chapter One -

THE PSYCHOLOGY
OF THE TRIANGLE

As a collegiate lacrosse player, I used to go to sleep at night concentrating on "the triangle." The triangle is the upper corner of the lacrosse goal cage, opposite the goalie's stick side. A shot placed in the triangle is near impossible to defend and results in a sure goal. Over and over again I would imagine myself shooting the ball into the triangle, just a fraction below the goal post. The attack players on our team called this the "psychology of the triangle."

Other sports, too, have a triangle. In tennis, a serve placed in the corner of the box (an imaginary triangle) at a high speed is nearly impossible to return.

A football pass placed in the corner of the end zone so only the receiver can catch it is another imaginary triangle. Again, perfect placement is near impossible to defend.

Other sports have key skills that can be improved through visualization.

My oldest son, Ben, and my daughter, Carly, are collegiate swimmers. They visualize their starts and turns in preparing for the race. My youngest son, Jackson, is an accomplished dancer and dance instructor – I watch him in amazement as he prepares his choreography, oftentimes visualizing his steps as he listens to music.

Later in life, I learned that this practice of mentally visualizing something, such as a score, is called "imagery." And today, many universities offer degrees in sports psychology, which does involve training in how imagery can improve athletic performance.

I have a specific memory of my senior lacrosse season. We, tiny Lafayette College, had home-field advantage against Penn State in the semi-finals of the NCAA Division I tournament. The night before the game, I repeatedly visualized a fake and score on a free eight-yard shot. It turned out that late in the first half a foul was called and I had an opportunity to execute the exact shot I had imagined. Rather than attempt to beat the goalie from eight yards out with the difficult triangle shot, I faked the shot, drawing all the defenders in front of me. I cut to the right of the defenders to score the triangle goal from a closer position and better angle. Exactly how I had imagined it!

More recently, it dawned on me that this same kind of sports imagery could be used to improve my attitude in all areas of my life. I began imagining how I would respond to the different stress-inducing situations in my life - the mess in the home office, the kids' text messaging, missed deadlines, last-minute school projects, hurtful comments, delayed traffic, fighting siblings - and how I would like to respond. Instead of imagining myself getting angry and silent, which would often be the case, I imagined an even-keeled and level-headed response that would bring about a positive change or level of acceptance. After all, the only person we can change is ourselves. And as these situations presented themselves, as they always will in all our lives, I was able to respond as I practiced.

The first time it worked, it felt like scoring the triangle goal in the Penn State game!

So, whether practicing for the big game or for difficult life situations, imagining a positive outcome and how to achieve it will bring a measure of success and peace to our lives.

SUZANNE DETAR

- Chapter Two -

FAMILY TRAITS

Observation suggests that athletic prowess is a family trait. Scientists may disagree if it's nature or nurture, but there is no doubt that certain behaviors seem to have been passed along the family tree. Take for instance Pro-bowl football quarterback Archie Manning's offspring – Peyton and Eli – both Super Bowl MVP quarterbacks.

And, of course, there is Ken Griffey, Jr, who surpassed the 600 career homerun mark, without the cloud of steroids. His famous father, Ken Griffey, Sr., was an all-star for the Cincinnati Reds in the late 1970s. Other athletic fathers and sons include father and French Open champion Yannich Noah and his son, Joakim, who won two national championships on the Florida Gator's basketball team before being drafted by the Chicago Bulls, and professional baseball player Bob Boone and his sons.

Other athletic siblings include tennis' Venus and Serena Williams, the four swimming Vanderkaays, who competed at the 2008 Olympic Trials, and professional and Olympic gold medal basketball players Reggie and Cheryl Miller (NBA and WNBA greats).

But it is not just athletic traits that get passed along. Obviously, we learn a lot of traits and behaviors from our families.

Sometimes these traits aren't so positive, such as nail-biting, alcoholism, too much television, bad nutrition and a host of others – you can name your own.

For me, while I did inherit the athletic trait from my family, I also inherited, learned or somehow developed our family characteristic of "stuffing." I'm not referring to over-eating. Like my Mom and my Grandmother and my Dad and his family, I have a negative behavior of keeping most of my emotions to myself.

When I started researching this Chapter, I thought it would be easy to come up with scores of famous athletic families. The truth is that there just are not that many famous-related athletes in proportion to the total number of professional or Olympic level athletes that compete at the top level of their sport.

What this dearth of athletic genetics confirms is that while there is a family connection to athletic performance, scientific studies have frequently found that performance is more shaped by training and motivation than by heredity. In other words, we can train and practice our way into good athletic performance even if Mom or Dad prefers Dickens and Shakespeare to Manning and Griffey.

The same is true for good emotional communication or any other family trait. Yes, there are family connections, either from nature (genetics) or nurture (socialization), but there is also individual responsibility and personal contribution.

Just like the athlete can train herself to world record time, we can train ourselves (sometimes with the help of the equivalent of a coach or mentor) to stop biting our nails, to communicate more effectively, to eat more healthy foods or to address whatever our family trait is that needs improvement. Again, insert your own here.

Two weeks ago I cut a paragraph and a half from a Chapter because I didn't want to share my feelings. Last week I cut a whole Chapter. Thanks to some gentle prodding from a friend, this week I wrote too much.

Proof positive that with a little effort and support, old family traits can be transformed.

SUZANNE DETAR

- Chapter Three -

NO BOUNDARIES

Most sports have physical boundaries. The goal line. The batter's box. The end line. The sideline. The baseline. The three-point line. The right field line. The starting line.

I always loved the game of women's lacrosse exactly because, before the 2006 rule change, there were no hard boundaries. Modeled after the way the American Indians played the game, the women's game was limited only by soft boundaries such as sloping hills, team benches, and stadium seating.

As a player, it was exhilarating knowing you were not constrained by a line. You were free to run and play hard, to stretch your limits and the limits of those around you.

If you ventured too far off into the soft boundary, the referee would blow the whistle and move the game back toward the center of the field. There was no loss of possession for going out of bounds. You were simply

15

gently reigned back in as the game clock continued to run.

I do remember a scary event at Rutgers University. We were playing the game on a football field, so were bounded not by the football sidelines but by the natural space designed as a playing field. The playing area was eventually bounded by a track that circled the grass field. While I do recall there were light poles for night games, we were playing during the day.

I played attack wing for Lafayette College and remember defending a Rutgers player as she brought the ball up field. Her eyes told me she was looking to pass to a player behind me who was cutting away from the center of the field toward the track area. Behind me, I heard a loud thud and the girl I was defending stopped playing, bringing her hand to her mouth in an obvious sign of shock.

A whistle blew, trainers rushed onto the field. An ambulance arrived.

The player behind me had run full speed into the light pole, never seeing it as she made her cut to the ball.

Sometimes not having boundaries can have significant negative impact, such as the head injury sustained by the Rutgers player when she collided with the pole.

But, also, sometimes not having boundaries can have just as important, but perhaps less obvious consequences.

The no-boundaries rule was eventually changed, not so much because of safety, but because of abuse. Players and coaches began to violate the spirit of the rule, using it not as an exhilarating and thrilling aspect of the game but as a way to stall and delay without penalty or loss of possession.

As a parent of three teens and as a recovering teenager myself, I know the safety dangers associated with lack of boundaries – alcohol and drug use, and other risky rule-stretching and thrill-seeking behaviors.

We have a natural tendency to push our boundaries beyond what is fair or healthy.

How often do we fail to set good boundaries in our own lives that often lead to injury and unfair play?

I was disappointed when, less than a week before the start of the 2008 Family Circle Cup, both Venus Williams and Justine Henin withdrew from the tournament due to injury. They are two of my favorite players and I silently wondered if they were really injured badly enough to warrant withdrawing from the tournament.

But, as I was running one Saturday morning and feeling an ache in my knee and heaviness in my calves, I slowed to a walk, saying to myself, "Better to slow down and walk than get an injury that will keep me from running at all."

I set a boundary with my own body. Then it dawned

on me. That is exactly what these two top, world-class athletes were doing. They were setting a boundary as to how far they would stretch the limits of their bodies against their commitment to the tournament and to their health for future events, including the summer's Grand Slams at the French Open and Wimbledon.

Seeing these top athletes set boundaries, and remembering my lacrosse days, served as a way to remind me to continue to set and enforce boundaries for myself and my children that keep the proper balance between exhilarating and safe.

It just might keep me, and them, from hitting a light pole.

- Chapter Four -

BREATHE EASY

When I was in fifth grade, I started taking saxophone lessons. I remember Mr. Simon teaching me the proper way to breathe – he laid down on a table, put a flute case on his stomach, and breathed through his diaphragm, making the flute case rise and fall at his abdomen.

I was totally grossed out by it.

But, now I realize that proper breathing is very important, not only in music, but in sport and life as well.

My youngest son took karate lessons with Sensei Glenn at Daniel Island Japan Karate Institute for several years. Sensei taught proper breathing with kiai.

During professional tennis action, you may have heard Maria Sharapova kiai-ing every time she hit the ball.

Both Sharapova and martial arts students use the kiai to amass energy and release a single explosive focus of energy. It is the coordination of breathing with the physical activity that creates the power. Scientific research and practical experience show that a relaxed and powerful exhalation can add power and stability to movement. Like Mr. Simon's breathing exercise, it involves the abdominal muscles and the diaphragm.

The kiai is also used to intimidate an opponent.

On a South Carolina Lowcountry note, it is akin to the "rebel yell."

Other proper breathing techniques can also improve performance. With weight lifting, exhaling through the exertions and inhaling as you relax the muscle reduces the chance of injury, makes lifting easier, and helps the athlete perform the exercise more efficiently.

If swimmers do not breathe properly in the pool, their times will increase as both increased breathing motion and improper breathing technique slow the movement through the water.

In recent years I've rediscovered Mr. Simon's technique from Yoga Journal's DVD instructor Patricia Walden. Each morning I put in my yoga DVD and breath and stretch with Patricia.

She encourages, "Observe your breath. Inhale and observe the ribs expand. Exhale. Feel the ribs moving back, very, very slightly."

It's both relaxing and invigorating at the same time.

"Normal inhalation. Slow, soft, deep exhalation."

I'm not looking to increase my times in any events yet, and I haven't hit the tennis courts in years, but the breathing does clear my mind so I can attack projects, dilemmas and everyday living with renewed vigor, confidence and peacefulness.

It's not likely you will hear a kiai coming from my office, but if you do, it will be more like a rebel yell, "It's past deadline!"

In which case, I probably didn't do my morning breathing and have lost my sense of peace.

SUZANNE DETAR

- Chapter Five -

GIVE YOUR BEST EFFORT

I don't like to do sit-ups, clean the litter box, run suicides or eat lima beans. And, in high school, I used to hate running "the square."

The Pottstown Sr. High School square - home to baseball fields, hockey fields, and lacrosse fields - was a large side-walked area that went around a grassy meadow-like space between the high school and the junior high. Our coaches usually started practice by requiring us to run one and three quarter times around the square. That was equivalent to a mile.

I actually hated running the square. Probably because I usually sprinted that mile.

The competitive nature inside me insisted that I never come in anything but first when running the square, even though it was only a warm-up – one exercise during part of one practice. When I got to college, I transferred this compulsion, during lacrosse and field hockey practice, to running suicides – battling each time not to come in second to my good friend, Debbie.

Always ringing in the back of my head during the square, or other drills, was my Dad's voice, "Practice like you play the game." In other words, practice hard. Hence, the sprint.

But by the time I got to college, it wasn't about coming in first as much as it was making sure I was giving it my best effort.

I've even transferred a little of that spirit to my work at the newspaper, sometimes being a bit compulsive about getting a better photo, writing a better article, and not getting scooped by other papers in the area.

Lately I've been doing some self-evaluation, introspection and exercise, and I'm feeling better, both physically and mentally.

Self-evaluation, when done honestly, isn't very fun either. In fact, I'd rank it right up there with sprinting the square.

Doing things we hate to do, with the effort they require, actually pays dividends. Just like practice.

Besides, who wants to live in a house that smells like a stinky litter box?

- Chapter Six -

DETACH FROM DISTRACTIONS

"Swing, batter, batter, batter, batter. Swing, batter, batter. Swing, batter, batter, swing."

"Pitcher's got a rubber arm."

That was Little League baseball trash talk back in the 1970s, usually intoned in a less than intimidating singsong voice.

Since then, distraction techniques executed by both fans and players have grown to new heights. Or, perhaps more appropriately described, trash talk has reached new lows in the age of YouTube and the quest for 15 minutes of fame.

Some of the most unique and memorable distraction methods occur when a basketball player is shooting foul shots. My earliest memories in this regard are attending high school playoff games when I was in middle school. We traveled to Reading, Pa. to watch the action on the courts in what I recall as a huge coliseum of a gym. When the players went to the foul line, the gym would slowly crescendo in a rumbling noise of feet stomping until it culminated in a deafening din of vibrating shoes on metal and wooden bleachers.

In a reverse-psychology technique, fans in the same gym would pull out the newspaper and get incredibly quiet and disinterested and hide their faces behind the paper as the players attempted to sink the free-throw.

Moving to football, in a not so long ago NFL season, poor Jessica Simpson was a victim of the nasty Dallas Cowboy fans' anger as they perceived her as a distraction to her then quarterback boyfriend, Tony Romo. I think there was even a movement to ban her from the ballpark.

The key for the athlete is not to get distracted. To stay focused on the game. To not even notice the distraction-inducing behavior.

But how? It is one thing to tell an athlete to ignore or not be distracted by a fan's antics, but is it something that can be taught?

Yes, according to a study published by the American Psychological Association in a December 2001 issue of the Journal of *Experimental Psychology: General*. In the study, the test group of novice golfers that was trained to perform with distractions performed better under pressure than two other test groups who were trained without distractions.

This got me to thinking about the possibility of improving my ability to block out the distracting behavior of people in my life.

I've recently learned that "detachment" is the term used to describe this kind of conduct - the behavior of not letting other people's antics be a distraction in our own lives. It is a mental assertiveness that allows us to put up and maintain boundaries, not to keep us from caring about people, but to keep us from being consumed by other people's demands on us.

Just like the athlete can't control the heckling fan, we can't control the troublesome behavior of people in our lives. And, just like the athlete, we can only control how we respond.

The athlete can improve her ability to block out the distraction. We, too, can learn to block out the distraction by giving up control over it.

Did we even realize that we were changing what we do because of the distracting behavior of other people in our lives? The basketball player who does that is likely to miss the shot.

Once we stop trying to control the distracter or to react to his behavior, we control our own shots.

I'm still working on improving my shooting percentage, particularly while under distraction.

SUZANNE DETAR

- Chapter Seven -

WORK YOUR WAY
OUT OF A SLUMP

"Slump? I ain't in no slump... I just ain't hitting."
- Yogi Berra

Yogi Berra might not have recognized his slump, but all avid baseball fans have agonized as they've watched their favorite player's batting average head toward the basement.

During the Boston Red Sox' 2013 World Series season, Boston's designated hitter, David Ortiz, faced 0-22 skid late in August. That's a slump. He didn't panic. His analysis at the time - "It happens. It's not the end of the world. I'll be back." And back he came, setting the World Series record books on fire, hitting 11 for 16 (.688) with two home runs and six RBIs against the Cardinals. He was also named the series MVP.

During the 2008 baseball season, then Seattle Mariner

Ichiro Suzuki carried the all-time highest career batting average for any player, raising his career average to .321 that season. But earlier that spring he was 0 for 21.

That's a slump. And most every hitter at every level of the game will face one at some point in his playing career.

He will try everything to get out of it. More practice in the batting cage. Adjusting his swing. Opening his stance. Closing his stance. Seeking more and different coaches. Viewing film of, and analyzing every aspect of his swing. Sleeping with his bat to improve their relationship. Anything to get out of the slump.

The player who wants out of the slump will even read and try what he finds on Web sites with sections entitled "slump busters."

But somewhere along the road, some players get discouraged and stop working on their swing. It might be in Little League, high school, Triple-A or "the bigs." Whenever it happens, the career is over.

Indeed, another Yogi truism makes the point: "Baseball is 90 percent mental and the other half is physical."

John Updike's *The Slump* brings that Yogism home. In the story, the batter ruminates about why he isn't hitting, blaming his slump on everything from slowing reflexes to paralyzing anxiety at the plate. And his slump has even spilled over into other aspects of his life, losing interest in his wife and not finding joy in things he once found fulfilling.

The Slump, to me, is really about feeling down and losing interest in life. Although it may or may not reach the point of clinical depression, it is a slump we can all get into from time to time depending on situations in our lives or on a chemical imbalance in our brains. And these kinds of slumps usually boil over into our personal relationships.

And just like the batter in a hitting slump, when we enter a life slump we need to work through it. Like David Ortiz, we need not panic.

We need to find our "slump buster."

Whether seeing a mental health professional, going on medication, confronting the situation, or recommitting to working on our relationships, doing something, as opposed to nothing, can help break the slump. Failing to do anything, on the other hand, leads to an end of some sort, just like the end of a ball career.

Several years ago, I recognized that I had entered a slump in many of my personal and work relationships. They were suffering from lack of good communication, unstated resentments, inattention, stuffed feelings and over-extension. Can anyone relate?

Having faced and worked on my relationship slump that year, I can attest that getting in the batting cage and working it out is more than worth the time and energy commitment.

My hitting is improving.

SUZANNE DETAR

- Chapter Eight -

BIG DECISIONS

When a professional athlete makes a decision to retire from a sport, it is a big decision.

In May of 2008, two top female professional athletes in their sport retired or announced their impending cessation of play. In the weeks leading up to her LPGA tournament at RiverTowne in Mt. Pleasant, SC, Annika Sorenstam declared her retirement. This wasn't totally unexpected as Annika, who had been battling back problems, had enjoyed a long and successful career. More surprising, however, was Justine Henin's immediate retirement from tennis. Only 25 and playing without injury, Henin was the first woman to retire while ranked No. 1 in the World.

I just couldn't imagine why she decided to retire just weeks before the French Open, an event she has dominated over the years and of which she was the three-time defending champion.

But then I saw her retirement announcement on TV and was so totally blown over by her ease, joy and contentment with the decision.

Henin said, "It's a great day in my life, I believe that you can call it that. I'm here today to announce to you that I am putting a definitive end to my tennis career... It's an end to a beautiful adventure."

Not all athletic retirements seem as calming or as thoughtful. Juxtapose the conclusion of Henin's professional tennis career with the pot-smoking-induced retirement of Miami Dolphin's running back Ricky Williams. Anyone watching his post-retirement interviews knew his decision-making was warped by drugs.

Other retirements, too, have left us scratching our heads. Michael Jordan's retirement from basketball to play baseball only to return to basketball again. Ditto for George Foreman, who retired from boxing as a young man only to return to the ring as a middle-aged bruiser.

All these retirement decisions got me thinking about how I make my own choices in life.

Like many of us, and perhaps a few of these sports retirees, I would often make a decision and then build an argument in support of my decision. After all, this backward process is how we are taught to justify decisions beginning as early as elementary school. It is engrained in our educations. Each of my three children has come home with persuasive writing assignments, such as why they need a cell phone. High school debate teams are assigned a position and build their arguments. Similarly, in law school, we were taught to build our arguments in support of our clients' positions.

Recently, I came across a thought-provoking statement in the book, *No Man Is an Island*, by Thomas Merton, an American monk. He wrote, "To make good choices, I must develop a mature and prudent understanding of myself and that will reveal to me my real motives and intentions."

So lately, when I have to make a decision, instead of making it and building an argument in favor of it, I delve into the real reasons behind it – I look at my real motives and intentions.

Shortly after this realization, I had to make a very difficult decision. In the past, I would have agonized and procrastinated and second-guessed the decision. But this time, I thoroughly analyzed my motivations and intentions and felt peaceful in knowing I was making the right choice for the right reasons. Yes, there was a list of pros and cons. But in the end, I sat down to truly examine and evaluate the driving force behind my decision. I asked myself, "Why am I really doing this?"

And like Henin, I've been able to find peace, joy, contentment and ease in that decision.

Life is a beautiful adventure.

SUZANNE DETAR

- Chapter Nine -

GOOD COMMUNICATION

"Lefty" Steve Carlton had Tim McCarver.

Bob Bryan has Mike Bryan.

Ekaterina Gordeeva had Sergei Grinkov.

Baseball. Tennis. Pairs figure skating.

These are examples of athletic pairs with amazing communication.

The all-time MLB left-handed strike-out leader, Steve Carlton, was traded to the Philadelphia Phillies from the St. Louis Cardinals in the early 1970s. A year later, his personal catcher, Tim McCarver, made his way to Philadelphia where he would receive Carlton's nasty slider. Carlton and McCarver had a communication unto themselves, even forcing the Phils to sit starting catcher Bob Boone every time Carlton came up in the rotation.

The Bryan brothers, in addition to being twins, are legendary tennis partners, having made the finals in seven consecutive men's doubles Grand Slam events. The brothers played on Daniel Island in 2004 when the Family Circle Tennis Center hosted Belarus in the Davis Cup. Their on-court communication and aggressive style of play was, and is, amazing to watch.

Gordeeva and Grinkov's communication on the ice was legendary. The movements of the 1988 and 1994 Olympic pair skating champions were perfectly in sync, their jumps huge and unbelievably beautiful. The duo married, had a child, and continued to express themselves as skaters until Grinkov died suddenly of congestive heart failure at just 28 years of age. Gordeeva's solo skate in honor of her husband and partner was chilling as she later said she felt as if she were skating with him.

The communication between these top performing athletes seems intuitive, as if they are engaging in an unspoken dialogue.

Maybe they were. But most likely, their smooth communication came from hard work and lots of practice.

In any event, I've learned that unspoken communication isn't communication at all. It's a recipe for misunderstanding.

For some of us, good communication comes easily. For others, it's an ongoing challenge.

How's your communication? Do you practice it? Or do you assume that other people should intuitively know what you're thinking?

Remember: The truth is that the only way people know what we want or expect from them is to tell them.

Open communication might not earn you an Olympic medal, a tennis championship or a strikeout record, but it just might earn you some peace of mind.

SUZANNE DETAR

- Chapter Ten -

THE NEW SEASON

It was only July, but yes, it was football season.

Sports pages, magazine covers, ESPN and other sports broadcasts were all focused on football. One of our advertising sales people said to me that he gets so pumped to see Clemson and USC football coverage dominating the sports section of the local daily paper.

While July is a little early, and still way too hot for me, I love football season. It conjures up for me cool weather, wearing sweatshirts, the smell of decomposing leaves and, yes, the "Fly, Eagles, Fly" fight song of my beloved Philadelphia Eagles.

Many of us love the changing of the sports seasons as much as we love the changing of the weather seasons. Fall means football, soup, sweatshirts and falling leaves. Winter means basketball, wrestling, skiing, snow shoveling and cozy snuggling by the fireplace. Spring ushers in flowers and baseball. And summer means hot weather, swimming, reading on the back porch, sunbathing at the beach and more baseball!

Reviewing some pages in my journal from this past winter, I found a reminder I wrote from a confidant who told me we all have different seasons in our lives. While I was struggling through a personal issue that seemed to make me self-absorbed, of which I was very well aware and very uncomfortable with, she reminded me that it was simply a season of my life.

Back then, and again as I reviewed my writings, I was immediately drawn to Ecclesiastes 3, which contains a philosophical discourse on the meaning of life.

And to many readers of my generation, it is the verse that Kevin Bacon uses to convince the pastor of the town in the movie *Footloose* that the kids should be able to dance: "To everything there is a season, and a time to every purpose under the heaven…"

Some seasons are winning seasons – in the mid-2000s the Phillies dominated the much locally loved Atlanta Braves, who, after having many, many winning seasons, were struggling in the NL East. Similarly, the seasons of our lives might feel like winning or losing seasons, depending on our own particular circumstances.

But like the verse from Ecclesiastes suggests, the seasons of our lives change just like the weather and just like the fortunes of the Phillies, Braves and Eagles.

It's also good to remember that even in the midst of a losing season, there are some plays that do make the highlight reel.

Another great idea to remember when things just don't seem to be going your way can be found in Pat Conroy's book, *My Losing Season*. In writing the memoir of his losing 1966-67 basketball season as a point guard for The Citadel, Conroy wrote of his team's 7-18 record, "There is no downside to winning. It feels forever fabulous. But there is no teacher more discriminating or transforming than loss."

Here's to a winning season and, at the very least, an appreciation of finding meaning in the lessons learned from loss.

And there is always the highlight reel if you need a little refresher.

SUZANNE DETAR

- Chapter Eleven -

IT JUST DOESN'T MATTER

Who remembers the irreverent but adorable Bill Murray character in the movie *Meatballs*?

I bought the DVD before vacation in hopes of viewing it with my daughter the night before we ran the 10th Annual Griffin 5K around Lake Mokoma in Pennsylvania. We did not have TV reception in our cabin but we could watch DVDs and VHS on our aging-cables-going-everywhere-one-of-a-kind-cabin-entertainment-system.

Correction, we could watch VHS.

We didn't get to watch the film as the DVD player kept telling us that "disk cannot be read" — which correlates directly with the theme of the film: "It just doesn't matter!"

Do you remember that scene? Summer camp counselor Bill Murray befriends Ruddy, the dorky middle-school boy who doesn't fit in and doesn't want to be at camp. At the end of the film, the "poor-kid" camp competes in a multi-day athletic competition against the "rich-kid" camp across the lake. The poor-kid camp always loses. But, this year could be different if Ruddy can "run like a rabbit" in a cross-country race that takes them through the woods. Hence, my motivation for the Griffin 5K.

But, in his wacky way, Bill Murray gathers the campers the night before the final race and delivers his Vince Lombardi motivational speech with the conclusion that, win or lose, it just doesn't matter. Murray beats the stone hearth with a log as the room erupts with the repetitive, "It just doesn't matter!"

My daughter, Carly, and I adopted that motto for the 5K. All we wanted to do was run our best race. Our goal was to finish the race. Winning or losing just didn't matter.

Sometimes, I'd like to tell my fellow parents of student-athletes (including reminding myself) that, in the scope of things, winning or losing the competition just doesn't matter. As a parent, and from my own memories as a student-athlete, I know this to be true.

After the 5K, I was lying on the cabin's back deck, letting the sun warm my bare feet as I rubbed out the soreness and contemplated what to write about this week – and that's when "It just doesn't matter" really came to me with meaning. I remembered a high school basketball playoff game where the score was a tight seesaw event.

With seconds remaining and the other team up by one point, I stole the ball from their point guard, sprinted down court and made a layup, putting us ahead by one point. On top of that, the other team committed a baseline violation on the ensuing inbound pass – turning the ball over to us with only a few seconds remaining.

A timeout was called and the feeling was amazing. I remember the joy and jubilation as the fans cheered and my teammates hugged me. All we had to do was inbound the ball on our end of the court and run the last few remaining seconds off the clock. The coach drew up a play to get the inbound pass to me with the instruction to run the clock down.

The ball came to me and as I dribbled to the side a girl from the other team stole the ball from me and made the winning goal at the buzzer.

As I sat in the sun, I remembered how devastated I was at blowing the game. But, I also realized I hadn't thought about it in well over 25 years. Hence, it just doesn't matter. Or, as a wise woman repeatedly told me during my growing up years, "You'll forget about it by the time you're married."

And she was right. I did forget about it. Only to be reminded about it 25 years later, as I also recalled the sometimes unhealthy pressure and importance both athletes and parents put on winning.

Carly beat me in the 5K, of course. Oh well, it just doesn't matter.

SUZANNE DETAR

- Chapter Twelve -

BEYOND SELF

To me, the best moment of the 2008 Summer Olympics didn't involve a world record or an amazing play. It didn't even involve a competition.

The defining moment of the Olympics came before an event even started. It occurred before the swimmers even got in the water for the women's 50-meter freestyle semifinal.

The race was broadcast live late on a Friday night, when many viewers had already tuned out for the night… and it came moments after Michael Phelps' 100-meter butterfly event, when he tied Mark Spitz' 7-gold medal record in a single Olympics in one of the most unusual finishes ever.

Even still, the ladies race was hyped-up because it involved 41-year old Dara Torres swimming her

50-meter semifinal. As Torres came out to swim her event that evening, she behaved in a manner inconsistent with personal preparation and focus. She started walking behind the blocks, talking to the other swimmers, and gesturing with her hands to hold off or stand down from the blocks. It was not the traditional focused demeanor of an athlete ready to swim. After talking to and motioning with her hands to the other swimmers, she walked behind her competitors to the side of the pool and spoke with the meet referee. At this point, the TV announcers were commenting on her odd behavior and how she was losing her focus on her event.

Moments later, the swimmer in the lane next to Torres, Swede Therese Alshammar, came rushing out from the locker room and raced up to the starting blocks. It turns out that Torres knew Alshammar's suit had torn moments before the event and asked the other swimmers and the meet referee to delay the start a few moments so her opponent could change her suit.

I couldn't recount the story to friends and family without tearing up.

That was the Olympic spirit at work. That was, to me, the Olympic moment of the 2008 Summer Games.

But, what is it about that situation that resonated so

emotionally with me?

Torres put fair competition above winning; she displayed an uncanny amount of poise and maturity, and she followed through by doing the right thing.

But again, why so compelling?

As I meditated on that question, the answer came more in the form of questions. Do I put fairness above other considerations in my relationships with family, friends and co-workers? Do I show poise and maturity in dealing with difficult situations? Do I do the right thing when faced with challenging circumstances? Do I see beyond myself?

To be honest, I can't answer "yes" to those questions all of the time. But what an awesome reminder it is to see someone looking beyond herself, especially in the most self-centered moment of an individual Olympic competition.

SUZANNE DETAR

- Chapter Thirteen -

REFOCUS

There are some lessons to be learned from those athletes who are able to refocus in the face of personal mistakes, bad officiating, or other unfair competition. But insight can also be gained from those who have difficulty getting their heads back in the game. Several examples from past Olympics come to mind.

USA veteran Olympic diver Laura Wilkinson, who won the gold medal in the 10-meter platform in the 2000 Sydney Olympics, was America's favorite, if not a long shot, at the Beijing Olympics. Married, in her 30s, and hurling her body off the equivalent of a three-story building over and over again had taken its toll on her physically. With taped wrists and triceps, Wilkinson over-rotated on her second and third dives in the final competition because the injuries prevented her from stopping her dive as she entered the water, essentially knocking herself from medal contention. Even with the injury, she was able to bounce on her second dive, a back 3½ somersault for which received scores ranging from 3.5 to 4.5, to close out her Olympic career with 8s and 9s on her final dive.

Speaking of diving, remember Greg Louganis' performance in the 1988 Seoul Olympics? Louganis hit his head on the springboard and suffered a concussion during the preliminary round. He was able to finish the prelims and eventually earned the gold medal while performing the same reverse 2 ½ pike that he flubbed so seriously in the earlier round of the competition. He displayed mental toughness in his ability to refocus after a terrible mistake – so much so that it earned him the Sports Illustrated Athlete of the Year moniker.

And in one of the most exciting nights of the Beijing Olympics (Phelps tying Spitz and Dara Torres' semifinal show of sportsmanship), beach volleyball players Rogers and Dalhausser pulled off an amazing victory after falling behind 0-6 to start the final set against the Swiss team. Displaying the ability to refocus and not dwell on their past mistakes, Rogers said he thought at the time that a comeback would be "gnarly." Gnarly indeed. The duo played on to win gold.

But gymnast Alicia Sacramone, who fell off the beam

as she attempted to mount the apparatus in the team event, couldn't shake the mistake as the team, only a point behind China, moved to the floor exercise. First up on the final event, Sacramone fell on a passing routine and stepped out of bounds on another move, two major guffaws.

After the event, she said, "I got a little nervous and I guess it carried over to the floor exercise...I tried to look over it but I guess it still followed me through."

Remember middle distance runner Mary Decker, who collided with Zola Budd in the 1984 Los Angeles games? Decker was a heavy favorite going into the games and was competing against Budd, who had made headlines for switching citizenship from the apartheid-banned South Africa to Great Britain just months before the games. Decker and Budd were leading but, after tangling feet, Decker fell and was unable to complete the race. Decker blamed Budd and still doesn't seem to have gotten over it.

And although not an Olympian, tennis bad boy John McEnroe got tossed from the Hall of Fame Champions Cup event he played in the states at the same time the Beijing Olympics were underway. For – what else? – yelling at an official and using vulgar language to question a call.

Have you ever been paralyzed by a past mistake you made, like Sacramone?

Have you ever suffered over and over again by bringing up unpleasant memories of past wrongs done to you, like Mary Decker?

Have you ever been so angry about a perceived wrong that you argued about it until it destroyed what it was you were trying to save, like McEnroe?

Of course, at one time or another, we all have had bad things happen to us, made terrible mistakes, suffered perceived wrongs, and felt that we were treated unfairly.

I'm working on being more like Wilkinson, Louganis and the Rogers/ Dalhausser team.

It's not easy, and maybe even a bit gnarly - but in the end, being able to refocus and let go of the past is truly the best victory.

- Chapter Fourteen -

LOOKING FOR PASSION

My youngest son Jackson is athletic.

But if he is not passionate about the sport in which he is engaged, I've found it can be tough for him to be motivated for practice, especially early morning practice.

Take swimming, for instance. When Jackson was ten years old he liked to swim. He even joined a year-round swim team late that summer. But, when it came time to get ready for an early morning swim practice… well, it was a challenge. There were a hundred reasons why he couldn't get out of bed or why he shouldn't swim on any particular morning.

Basketball was a different story. At age 10, he was always ready for basketball practice and wanted to arrive early. He'd shoot hoops in the driveway and with the neighbor kids. He had some passion for basketball.

But that passion is nothing like when he is involved in hip-hop dance. Even back when he was 10, he called his instructor, Miss Angel, for extra practice hours. He practiced flips and handsprings every chance he got, he wanted to arrive early, and he even drew pictures of dance and gymnastics.

I've seen this same passion in my other children. Carly has passion for basketball. Ben for swimming.

Have you seen this passion in your kids? Your co-workers?

Yourself?

Why or why not?

I remember watching a short profile on Mike Smith, the then head coach for the Atlantic Falcons. Both video and audio followed him from pre-game practice, through the game, to the post game locker room. I was absolutely blown away by his passion for his job. It wasn't necessarily passion for football. Instead, the profile showed a man who had a passion for teaching and for people...and it was obvious that his players really followed and respected him. Heck, two minutes of learning about the guy and I wanted to follow him.

I've seen that passion in another football coach and teacher. Rick was our neighbor and friend in the last neighborhood we lived and is a high school football coach and P.E. teacher. We went to most of his games and always had so much fun after the games hanging out with him, his coaches, the other teachers and their spouses. These were people who were passionate about teaching and coaching.

Do you face your days like Jackson faced his early morning swim practice, with grumbles and complaints? Or do you face it like he faced gymnastics and dance, with joy, commitment and passion?

I confess, I was the first one to get frustrated by his swim complaints...yet I often fall into the same rut - complaining instead of doing.

And ruts can be deep and wide and difficult to get out of. To live with passion requires effort and, sometimes, courage to climb out and get back in the groove.

If we are involved in something that doesn't ignite our passion, why not try something else or try something new?

Get up and find the passion.

SUZANNE DETAR

- Chapter Fifteen -

ISOLATION

My daughter, Carly, played volleyball in middle school. I can remember especially enjoying watching her Daniel Island Middle School seventh and eighth grade volleyball team defeat CE Williams in one of the best matches they played that year. The girls won the first two games, each by a very close score, to take the match.

There were some amazingly long points, which was a treat for the spectators. But even more enjoyable was watching the girls grow from single hits across the net from early in the season to multiple hits and sets. The players were no longer isolated individuals on the court, but were teammates working together to set and score.

That particular volleyball match came just days after Terrell Owens slammed his team and his quarterback, Tony Romo and the Dallas Cowboys, for not giving him the ball enough in their 2008 loss to the Washington Redskins. Meanwhile, Owens' number was actually called on one third of all of Dallas' plays in that game.

Owens' attitude was totally the opposite of team play. He is the ultimate example of why there is no "I" in the word "Team." And when the "I" becomes too large, it leads to loss and isolation and a whole lot of bad feelings among teammates. This affliction, which I've dubbed the "T.O. Syndrome" infected his teams in San Francisco, Philadelphia and Dallas.

Thinking back to earlier games of the volleyball season, I remembered a third and final deciding game where the team blew a big lead and lost the match. During that final game, the players became tense, forgetting about setting, and trying to score the kill on individual hits. They became alone and isolated on court even though they were surrounded by their teammates in a gym filled with fans.

It was akin to the batter in a baseball game who tries to bring his team back with one big swing, forgetting that just getting on base one hitter at a time is what wins games.

It was a minor version of the T.O. Syndrome.

We all can get in this panic mode at times, especially when under stress. And then we become isolated like the individual players on an athletic squad.

And just like T.O. and the Daniel Island Middle School Volleyball team, we need to remember we are not in it alone, but have family and friends to bring us out of isolation.

SUZANNE DETAR

- Chapter Sixteen -

ANXIETY-REDUCING MANTRAS

A sports mantra is defined as "an intervention strategy by athletes to focus attention internally and to reduce anxiety."

I've utilized several different mantras over the years to assist me through workouts and/or competitions. My most recent jogging mantra is not very inspiring. I inhale through the nose and count, "4, 5, 6"; exhale through the nose and count, "1, 2, 3." This mantra was born from a temporary pass code I had to memorize and, because I needed to learn it at the start of a recent attempt to train for a 5K, it has stuck. When I feel my breathing becoming uneven or difficult to catch, I instinctively revert to my mantra and, within a few repetitions, feel myself come back to center and back to a relaxed breathing pattern.

Over the years, my running, swimming, biking, yoga or competitive mantras have taken on religious tones, angry rebellious tones (doesn't work well), peaceful chants, and motivating song lyrics.

The "4-5-6, 1-2-3" mantra is not very inspiring. But it has proven personally effective.

My "God is good, you can pass her. God is good, you can pass her. God is good, you can pass her" mantra might be a bit more inspiring. It was to me when I competed in my first (and only) sprint triathlon, the 2003 Family Circle Tennis Center Triathlon.

Sport's mantras actually evolved from a method borrowed from Buddhism and Hinduism, both of which utilize the mantra as a technique for spiritual advancement. Mantras are an integral part of any yoga practice, as the literal translation means "instrument of thought" or "to free from the mind."

In trying economic times, who wouldn't like to free his or her mind from worrying about paying the bills or losing a lifetime's worth of retirement security? What parent couldn't use a little cerebral clearing when it comes to the anxiety, stress and worry caused by raising children, especially teenagers?

I've found that my sports mantras are good to use to focus attention and reduce the tension of everyday life's stressors. Whether during stressful work situations or anxiety inducing home dilemmas, I often find my breathing, stress and tenseness hitting the same levels of exhaustion and difficulty that occurs during running or other physical activity.

A "God is good" mantra or even a one word mantra like "peace" or "relax," when I remember to use it, often brings the stress and anxiety levels down and the breathing back to normal. This not only relaxes me, but my family as well.

Mantras – a good way to reduce anxiety on and off the athletic field.

SUZANNE DETAR

- Chapter Seventeen -

BAD CALLS

What do you do when someone else's mistake becomes a problem for you?

Take, for instance, NFL referee Ed Hochuli's game-deciding mistake in Denver several years ago that turned a likely win for San Diego into a last-minute loss. Hochuli blew the whistle ending the play in which Denver quarterback Jay Cutler clearly fumbled on 2nd-and-1 at the 1-yard line. San Diego recovered the fumble and would have been able to let the clock run and secure the victory. But because Hochuli had blown the play dead, Denver kept the ball and scored on an ensuing play to win the game.

Everyone involved, including Hochuli, admits it was a mistake. It was a bad call.

The San Diego coaches and players were forced to

accept the mistake and the negative consequences it brought to team.

I'm sure we have all been in situations where someone else's mistake became a problem for us. I know I sure have.

In these situations, it is helpful to remember that it is one thing to find something unacceptable. It is entirely another thing to determine what to do about.

The bad call has been made and it can't be overturned or changed. In the football example, it was a judgment call that was not reviewable under the then current NFL review rules, which provided that the ball cannot change possession after the whistle is blown.

San Diego's Norv Turner did what most coaches would do. He complained. And, at most, complaining puts the referee on notice and may make them think carefully before the next decision.

But even more importantly, the league has a system in place to review all the calls and to rate the officials after each game. The Hochuli call was not only reviewed, but the league also reviewed and is reconsidering changing the rule about whether that type of call should be reviewable on the field and whether possession can change after the whistle is blown.

How many of us rant and rave over a problem but do little afterwards to ensure the same thing doesn't happen again? But, like the blown call in sports, ranting and raving at someone who has hurt or offended us may bring about temporary change but it really doesn't do much good.

We have to accept the mistake and its impact and move on. That doesn't mean we submit to a degrading situation or accept the unacceptable. It means accepting the fact of a situation and then deciding what to do about it.

It means, like NFL football, that we have good system of review and analysis and, if necessary, we can initiate an effective response and effect change.

Don't let bad calls keep you out of the game.

SUZANNE DETAR

- Chapter Eighteen -

EXPECTATIONS

Peyton Manning was the 2013 *Sports Illustrated* Sportsman of the Year. Would he succumb to the *SI* cover jinx?

Jameis Winston of Florida State is was the 2013 Heisman Trophy winner. Could he tank as many Heisman winners before him have?

While Manning has already exceeded his own and other people's expectations, each year a quarterback, especially an aging one, is put under new and additional scrutiny. Similarly, Winston, then a freshman, still had a lot to prove to those who had high expectations of him.

Manning and Winston aren't the only athletes to face high expectations. Think about the first-round draft pick with the huge signing bonus, or other *SI* cover athletes and Heisman Trophy winners, or those football players who have graced the cover of EA Sport's Madden NFL football video games.

In 2013, Josh Hamilton became a 100-plus multimillion dollar paid star with the Los Angeles Angels. As a Texas Ranger he mesmerized baseball fans at the 2008 All-Star game by hitting a record 28 homeruns in the first round of the Home Run Derby. But this first-round baseball pick with ties to the lowcountry was considered a lost cause with unfulfilled expectations just a few years ago. Drafted No. 1 in 1999 by the Tampa Bay Devil Rays, Hamilton's fast start in the minors with the Charleston RiverDogs came to a halt as he battled drug problems and subsequent drug-related suspensions in the 2004, 2005 and 2006 seasons.

Sports psychologist Jim Loehr explains the *SI* cover jinx and under-performances for others with high athletic expectations, such as Heisman winners, franchise players, and first round draft picks, as "a failure to efficiently metabolize heightened expectations."

I kind of see it as the pressure cooker exploding.

Expectations create a lot of pressure.

Have you ever felt like Josh Hamilton or Jameis Winston might feel as they face the high expectations their past athletic achievements demand for their future? Have you ever felt as if you couldn't attain the expectations placed on you? Have you ever felt that people have high expectations for you that seem unattainable?

Lately, I've felt the pressure of other people's expectations. I'm reminded of how expectations can dominate, cripple or propel our actions.

Some expectations of some people I simply won't embrace. Those expectations I recognize as unreasonable. But other expectations are a privilege to embrace.

Several years ago, Billy Jean King told Maria Sharapova as she stepped on the court in the Australian Open final that "pressure is a privilege."

We can embrace the pressure of acceptable expectations and propel ourselves to meet our goals or we can avoid, deny or quit. I'm looking for ways and opportunities to metabolize this year's expectations.

SUZANNE DETAR

- Chapter Nineteen -

UNRESTRAINED JOY

I can just picture the memory in my mind: six eight and nine-year-old boys parading another boy of similar age around the gym on their shoulders – smiles etched across each face. This is my image of unrestrained joy.

Only minutes before this jubilant parade, there was another moment of unrestrained joy. These same eight and nine-year-old teammates worked the basketball in to their small teammate, who turned and scored a basket. The players erupted into human pogo-sticks, celebrating the boy's first, and only, basket of the season.

Unrestrained joy is itself a joy to see. Their smiles spread to my face and I, too, turned into a pogo-stick, along with a gymnasium full of parents.

Yet somehow, as a side effect to adulthood, we forget how to experience joy and our overflowing feelings of happiness get relegated to rare instances of contagious behavior brought on by the youth around us. Perhaps it's because we have witnessed joy perverted into cockiness, especially on the professional football field. Instead of unrestrained joy, we see a prideful display of self-centeredness. A linebacker flexing and strutting and pounding his chest as he taunts the quarterback he just sacked. A wide-receiver gyrating or trying to come up with the next shenanigan that will give him air time on the highlight reel.

As a result, some of us experience an opposite attitude – an attitude of repressed joy. Not wanting to appear cocky, we suppress our gleeful feelings. Instead of celebrating, we keep our happiness hidden under a bushel, failing to "let it shine," as the children's song teaches.

Joy can and should be contagious. When we witness it, it fills us with unexplained emotion – it connects us to one another.

When we experience and show spontaneous and natural emotions of great delight ourselves, we share the gift of joy with others.

I'm learning. It's not cocky to experience unrestrained joy. Instead, it's a blessing to pass it on.

- Chapter Twenty -

MOMENTS IN TIME

One of the most intriguing, telling, and descriptive ways to tell a sports story is through the camera lens. My favorite photo to capture is the reaction shot. A reaction shot is a photograph of fans, players or coaches responding to the play or outcome.

If the photo is of players joyously giving their coach a Gatorade bath, the reader knows that the team won or performed a significant feat. The photographer has captured that moment in time - the joyful celebration that accompanies a win.

I once took a photograph of tennis star Dinara Safina moments after her defeat in the finals of the 2007 Family Circle Cup to Jelena Jankovic. She slouched on the courtside bench with a towel across her legs. The reaction shot depicted the dejection of loss.

We all, like these athlete examples, have emotional moments in time. Sometimes our faces and body language show pain, joy, love or a host of other emotions.

But these moments are simply that – moments. Our lives are not defined by these individual moments. More often than not, the true story is what we do after these moments in time. Safina regrouped after the moment the photo was captured, accepted her runner-up trophy and check, and spoke to the Family Circle crowd in a most humorous and generous fashion, and went on to win, and lose, many more tennis matches.

A danger arises when we form unfair and limited judgments from the moments we catch in other people's lives, or even of our own, either from a photo, from a short term experience, or from an intense involvement.

While a moment in time can give us insight into ourselves and others, we must be vigilant not to let them become the basis of our judgments.

Simply seeing Safina's dejection contradicted her humor and generous gift of good sportsmanship. Sometimes, we have to stick around beyond mere moments to learn the whole story.

- Chapter Twenty-one -

STAY ON YOUR FEET

I don't have a foot fetish. Yet, as I watched tennis at the 2009 Family Circle Cup, my eyes and thoughts kept turning to feet.

Actually, I was focused on moving feet.

The players' footwork was off at times – Venus Williams fell twice in her opening round match, runner-up Caroline Wozniacki took a tumble in her semi-final match against Elena Dementieva, and Vera Zvonareva had to be carried off the court after her tournament-ending fall.

These women discovered that if they didn't keep their feet moving, they were going to fall down.

As I watched Wosniacki and Sabine Lisicki warm-up for their finals match, I remembered a time when, as a field hockey player, I didn't keep my feet moving. Well, actually, I didn't move them at all, and I ended up flat on my back. I was playing in my first collegiate field hockey game, Millersville State had secured the push-back to start the game, and as the inner-forward I was lined up over the ball. Moments after the push-back, the Millersville girl (a true monster-sized player compared to my then diminutive 118 pound frame) ran right over-me. I was stunned. I was embarrassed. And it hurt.

Lesson learned. Keep your feet moving.

But, sometimes our falls or mistakes come when we are moving too fast. Again, from field hockey, as a forward I often had wide-open breaks to goal. Yet, somehow, and all too often, I would get my feet moving faster than the ball and end up tripping over the ball.

Isn't life like that? Sometimes, we are going too slow and other times, too fast?

Either way you look at it – keep moving or slowing down. It's about staying on your feet, getting up when you fall and staying in the game.

- Chapter Twenty-two -

MISTAKES

My children once had a wonderful first grade teacher who told them, "A mistake is only a mistake until you fix it."

At the time, I thought it was insightful advice, and, for the most part, I still do. And I'm looking forward to reading a book I discovered while researching this article: *Mistakes worth making: how to turn sports errors into athletic excellence.*

Of course, mistakes are opportunities to learn and grow.

But let's face it, sometimes mistakes are beyond repair.

For example, in basketball if the player commits a traveling infraction, it is a turnover and loss of possession. The mistake cannot be fixed for that occasion. True, the player should learn from his mistake and realize he has to dribble before he can run with the ball. If a player continually makes the traveling infraction, causing his team to lose the ball over and over again, the coach will pull the player from the game. Eventually, the player either learns to dribble when running with the ball or finds another sport or endeavor to explore.

What do we do when we, or the people we love, can't seem to learn from their mistakes? How long should we leave the player in the game who continues to travel, causes multiple turnovers, and hurts the team? How long do we pour energy into a failing business, stay in an abusive relationship, cover for an underperforming colleague or pursue an endeavor where we consistently fail?

Sometimes a mistake is a mistake. And as much as we want to try to make it right, it's just not possible.

But that doesn't mean we need to be pessimistic, depressed or downtrodden about it.

Sometimes mistakes can be opportunities to move forward in a new direction.

To start a new business, to pick up a guitar, to go on a date, to learn to crochet, to get in shape, to change jobs, to write a book, to explore your heart's desire.

Even unfixable mistakes create new opportunities to expand our life experiences.

Yes, a mistake is only a mistake until you fix it…except when it is unfixable, and then it is an opportunity to grow.

- Chapter Twenty-three -

MUSCLE MEMORY
& POSITIVE AFFIRMATION

An important concept in athletic training is muscle memory. Muscle memory is developed through an exercise routine based largely on repetitive motion. But, for muscle memory to be truly effective, it is crucial that the exercise program be accurate. Otherwise, the muscle commits to memory an inefficient and/or damaging motion.

We've all seen people running in awkward positions. And although we might not identify it as poor muscle memory, that is indeed what deficient running form is all about.

While training for a Mud Run and as part of our weekly workouts at my local CrossFit gym, we often practiced running form. Many of us have been running and competing in athletic events for years, and it seemed odd to practice running form – something so familiar.

But many of us, including me, were not keeping proper, efficient form. As we worked on form, I felt my efficiency and stamina improve. But, I noticed, as I became fatigued, I reverted back to my old, improper form as my old muscle memory took hold – mainly standing upright and not leaning to let gravity pull me forward.

It was during one of these workouts that I realized that I tend to do this with other, non-athletic memories as well. Perhaps you do too.

The brain has been referred to as our largest muscle. And if we have been exercising it with negative thoughts, those are the thought forms we have, especially when we are tired and fatigued. That's why positive affirmations and optimistic thinking help pull us from damaging thoughts that we may have developed throughout our lives. It's also why it isn't wise to make big decisions when we are mentally fatigued.

At first glance, the thought of positive affirmations may seem as odd as a star track athlete practicing running form, but oh how effective it can be! That is what repetitive training is all about.

We can reprogram our thinking just as we've reprogrammed our running muscles.

My new running mantra on form has been "lean, lean, fall, fall." A new brain mantra based on a positive affirmation may also be in order. I'm working on it.

Are you ready?

- Chapter Twenty-four -

ADD A LITTLE CONFUSION

I was addicted to the P90X infomercials that were regularly featured on TV during the first decade of the 21st Century and beyond. Of course, the 90-day transformation stories are motivating and dramatic. I find the concept of muscle confusion, a core element in the P90X exercise program, intriguing. In the last Chapter, I wrote about muscle memory and proper form. And although muscle confusion may seem to be a conflicting principle to muscle memory, it actually pertains to a different concept altogether.

Muscle memory is about doing each exercise efficiently and with proper form. Muscle confusion promotes doing a variety of exercises (always with proper form).

The theory of muscle confusion is that you will have greater results if your workouts have variety in them.

On the P90X program's Web site, muscle confusion is explained as a training method "which accelerates the results process by constantly introducing new moves and routines so your body never plateaus, and you never get bored!"

Regularly changing your workouts encourages your body to adapt to new routines and to become stronger in new areas, the theory teaches.

The muscle confusion principle may be open to debate among different fitness gurus. One point that rings true, at least for me, is that mixing up the workout keeps me interested and excited and it forces me to try exercises that I haven't done before.

I don't do the P90X program, but I do most of my training through CrossFit workouts. Although not billed under the muscle confusion moniker, the workouts are varied and continually push me and all the members of the class to extend our comfort zones and to take on new exercises (clean, jerk, burpees) and weights (dead lifting our bodyweight) that some of us have never tried before, or haven't done since we were kids (pencil rolls and pull-ups).

The muscle confusion principle could be extended to our ordinary life activities. Mixing it up can keep us fresh and interested. If we try things outside our regular comfort zone, we become stronger in new areas.

For instance, I generally do not like to go into social settings by myself, yet as I've started to do it with a bit more frequency, I find that I have adapted to it. I am also less anxious and have become more and more comfortable doing it.

The same is true in my work life – adding a variety of new job responsibilities keeps me fresh and interested.

Where could you add some confusion to your life?

SUZANNE DETAR

- Chapter Twenty-five -

MORE THAN THE GAME ITSELF

When my son, Ben, was in high school, I would go watch him swim for the City of Charleston Southern Marlins Racing Team.

At one particular meet, I was happy to see that my neighbor, Gina, was there to watch. Gina, who works for a physical therapy center and swam in college in the 1980s, was there to offer support for a former patient, a senior swimmer who was recovering from a shoulder injury. Each time the young woman was in the pool, Gina watched and cheered. And after each event, she offered the girl words of encouragement and stroke analysis.

I enjoyed sitting with Gina and catching up with her about her own children. But I enjoyed even more witnessing the impact she was having on that young swimmer's life.

Yes, the technique instruction was helpful. Yet, the true teaching happening that day was the impact she was having by showing a young woman that adults other than her parents care about her.

How fortunate we are if we've had a Gina in our lives. Some of us may have had that particularly awesome coach or a family friend who supported and taught us lessons beyond the athletic field. For me, I'm amazed that my elementary school best friend's father came out to watch me play baseball on a regular basis. What a gift of caring that has lasted and makes me feel worthwhile and cared about more than thirty years later!

What are we doing to build up the teens, children or other adults in our circle of influence?

For teens in particular, are we aggravated that they are boisterous, drive too fast, and seem unappreciative of the advantages they have in their lives? Do our actions and facial expressions communicate our disapproval?

As coaches or teachers, do we only care about the performance results?

Or do we see beyond the exterior of the teen's defenses, beyond the results of their athletic performance, and strive to encourage and build them up?

Gina's example and our own memories can be gentle reminders that teaching and coaching offer benefits well beyond the game itself.

- Chapter Twenty-six -

TAKE RESPONSIBILITY

In 2010, the two time defending National League Champions, the Philadelphia Phillies, were known for their overpowering offense and hustle.

But as the 2010 season wore on, both had been nonexistent, until one Saturday following a very lackluster performance.

During this particular weekend, the Phillies battled it out with their divisional rivals, the New York Mets. In Friday night's first game of the series, the Mets clobbered the Phils, 9-1. In the fifth inning of that game, Philadelphia's centerfielder, Shane Victorino, failed to run out a dropped third strike by the Mets' catcher. That's the kind of lackluster hustle that kills a team and was so very unlike the gritty "Flyin' Hawaiian's" (Victorino's nickname) normal attitude.

After the game, he apologized to the fans and his teammates for his lack of hustle and said it wouldn't happen again. The following night he hit a three run homer to help blank the Mets 10-0, and in the last game of the series, he hit a grand slam home run as the Phillies took two of three games from the Mets and climbed back into first place of the division.

We can learn from how Victorino took responsibility for his mistake, forgave himself and moved on.

How often do we make excuses for our mistakes, rationalizing away our behavior with one justification or another? Victorino could have made the excuse that he would have been out anyway or that they were out of the game so it didn't matter. But he didn't. Instead, he admitted he was wrong.

Some of us may not have difficulty admitting our mistakes. Instead, we beat ourselves up for our mistakes, making it almost impossible to move forward. Victorino was clearly upset with himself for not playing hard, but he went out the next two nights and played like the Gold Glove, hard-hitting speedster who helped lead the Phillies to victory so many times before.

Moving forward in a positive direction after making mistakes, like Victorino did in this situation, reminds me of encouragement found in Barry Sear's book *The Zone*. *The Zone* teaches a healthy way of eating, but just as important as the nutritional plan itself, the book reminds us that if we eat outside of the zone, consuming unhealthy or large portions, it's okay, we can get back in the zone at our next meal.

Whether it's playing ball, cheating on our nutritional plan, dealing with a stressful family situation or resolving a work problem, accepting responsibility for our actions, forgiving ourselves, and moving forward is the best course of action. In the end, we can all learn a valuable lesson from a ball player who turned a lack of hustle into a resurgence of sorts.

SUZANNE DETAR

- Chapter Twenty-seven -

HANDLE THE CURVE

Life can throw us curveballs at times. It's how we handle the curve that can make all the difference in our lives.

That's the theme of a fictional book by Joseph Wallace, *Diamond Ruby*. Best known for his non-fictional baseball histories, Wallace's *Diamond Ruby* is a fictional story inspired by organized baseball's first female pitcher, 16-year-old Jackie Mitchell, who struck out Yankee greats Babe Ruth and Lou Gehrig on only seven pitches in 1931. She was later banned from the sport by Judge Kenesaw Mountain Landis, baseball's first commissioner, who deemed the game "too strenuous" for women.

But the book is not a feminist anthem. Rather, it is a book that weaves the excitement and lifestyle of baseball, boxing, and Coney Island, with the realities and challenges of the flu epidemic of 1918 and life on the streets of New York City for the down and out in the Roaring Twenties.

And although the main character in the book is an amazing fastball thrower, the story is more about how she reacts to curveballs that come her way, including losing most of her family to the flu epidemic at age 13, leaving her with the responsibility to raise her two young nieces. Her "freakish" ability to throw a baseball allows her to befriend Babe Ruth and Jack Dempsey, two characters who come alive in the book, but she soon gets caught up in a web of conspiracy and deadly threats from Prohibition rum runners, the Ku Klux Klan, and the gangster underworld.

Ruby is continually faced with making decisions about her and her nieces' survival. When she learns the commissioner is going to ban her from baseball, a sport which provides her with her sole source of income for feeding her family, she momentarily starts to feel sorry for herself, but, as the book explains:

"[Ruby] already lived too long to allow herself to succumb to self-pity. It didn't get you anywhere. It merely slowed your mind. There was always a strategy, a solution. You just had to learn all the facts, and then you could put them to use."

What a great life philosophy. I saw it in action once

at a youth swim meet. During warm-ups, Logan, a ten-year-old swimmer, was accidentally smashed in the eye and nose by an older male swimmer's elbow. The eye immediately turned black and blue and was very tender, making it impossible and too painful to wear her goggles for her races. But, rather than wallow in self-pity and refuse to swim, Logan found a different style of goggle, one that made contact on her face further outside of her eye socket, and she raced to some of her personal best times at the meet.

When curveballs come our way, let's not let our minds be slowed by self-pity. Let's learn the facts and find a solution. Just like Logan...and just like Ruby.

SUZANNE DETAR

- Chapter Twenty-eight -

POSITIVE SELF-TALK

Sports psychologists and researchers have studied the benefits of positive self-talk in a variety of athletic movements and under a variety of self-talk conditions.

The research concludes that positive self-talk increases athletic performance – the level of improvement varies depending on, among other things, the type of self-talk and the type of athletic skill measured.

I've always used self-talk as a motivational component of my workouts – repeating such phrases as, "You can do it," "Yes we can," and even borrowing the Nike motto "Just do it."

Without realizing it, I was practicing motivational self-talk. And, when I was able to talk to myself in positive language that encouraged me to complete a task, I was indeed motivated to do it and to push myself to greater performance levels.

But as I researched this Chapter, I discovered that performance was increased even greater for athletes when they used instructional self-talk. It is a method that involves telling yourself what to do during the course of the athletic maneuver.

You may have experienced a particular exercise that gives you difficulty. I have two: pull-ups and handstands.

I used to have a huge mental block at performing these exercises, but, through motivational self-talk, I am able to persevere through them. But I'd like to do more than persevere. I want to excel.

With pull-ups, for example, I now know and believe that if I can talk myself through the proper pull-up form (for example, kicking my legs back to increase my forward momentum) that my performance should increase.

The same research is also confirmed outside of sports and in many areas of our lives. Positive self-talk, both motivational and instructional, improves our skills in a variety of actions and relationships.

Whether it's expending and developing an everyday skill such as cooking or confronting that difficult family member or coworker, positive self-talk can make all of our endeavors a more successful experience.

You can do it!

- Chapter Twenty-nine -

LEARN TO BE RESILIENT

If you've ever been to a little league soccer or football game, a middle school basketball game, a high school volleyball game, a swim meet, a professional football game, a collegiate baseball game – or to just about any sporting event at any level - you've most likely witnessed a player get frustrated and discouraged. You've also probably witnessed her inability to shake it off negatively affect the rest of her performance. Most likely, you've also seen athletes of every age and every level battle back.

Some athletes bounce back. Others need to work on readjusting their mindset.

That's where resiliency comes in.

An article on www.usaswimming.org teaches about resiliency in the context of swimming. Aimee Kimball, Ph.D., a sports psychologist at the University of

Pittsburgh, explains that "resilience is simply readjusting."

A memorable example of a team readjusting to bounce back to victory was the Philadelphia Eagles' big "come from behind" win over the New York Giants in 2010. Down 31-10 to start the fourth quarter, the Eagles readjusted to pull off the amazing 38-31 punt return for the victory as time expired.

On the other hand, I've seen swimmers leave a meet early after swimming only one or two events because they were so discouraged by their early swims that they just gave up.

Kimball cautions athletes not to turn every mistake, setback or challenge into a drama. Yes, disappointment in a loss or a poor performance is expected, but don't treat it as the end of the world, she notes. Rather, she writes, "...view the setback as a challenge that can make you stronger, more motivated and mentally tougher."

Kimball encourages athletes to work on their resiliency (it's something you can learn and improve upon) and she gives this advice: "...After a race, regardless of the outcome you may want to make a habit of asking yourself three questions, 1) What did I do well?, 2) What can I improve on for next time?, and 3) What is my physical and mental plan for my next event?"

This is good advice for our life's struggles outside of the pool and off the field as well.

Do you tend to overdramatize a personal setback? To focus on the negativity of a situation? To be paralyzed with fear of the uncertainty of a proposed action?

We can all learn how to be more resilient by asking Kimball's three questions in our own personal situations, and by focusing on the positive, seeking ways to improve, and creating a plan for the future.

To read Kimball's full article, visit www.usaswimming.org.

SUZANNE DETAR

- Chapter Thirty -

RELIABLE

Are you someone that people can count on?

A recent online advertisement recruiting softball players for a successful competitive team had as the number one requirement in the ad – "must be reliable."

It wasn't "must have strong throwing arm," "must be home run hitter," "must be fast," or any other "must" regarding athletic ability.

Similarly, one of my favorite athletes isn't necessarily a person, but a position – the sixth man in basketball. And my favorite sixth man of all time is Bobby Jones, who played for the Philadelphia 76ers when Julius Erving (Dr. J) was the team leader. When Jones came on the court to give Dr. J, Moses Malone, or Daryl Dawkins a breather, the coach, the fans and the other players knew they were going to get a gigantic effort from Jones.

One of the coolest things about great sixth men, and Jones most particular, is that they are so reliable. They may not be the greatest athlete on the court, they may not have great showmanship, they may not have charisma, but the sixth man is the player who gives it his all for the time he is on the court. He is reliable, or he wouldn't be the sixth man.

Jones reportedly wasn't passionate about basketball (he loved track and field), but Dean Smith liked the way he played the game and recruited him to play college ball for UNC under scholarship. Despite his lack of love for the game, Jones played every minute on the court with great effort, saying in a 1983 interview, "When I'm in there, I just play as hard as I can. In the Bible, it says we're supposed to give 100 percent in whatever it is we do—and that's what I do."

Do you give your best effort at home, at work, or with your other endeavors?

Do you give 100 percent?

Are you a good sixth man?

- Chapter Thirty-one -

CONTROL ISSUES

There are a lot of control issues in sports.

A basketball coach, when scheduled to play a team that has a lot of speed and an amazing fast break, will take practice time to teach his players to "control their fast break." He will institute plays designed to slow the pace of the game. His game plan is to control the other team's strength.

In tennis, Roger Federer's opponents try to pin him on the backhand side of the baseline so he can't come to mid-court and unleash those geometrically uncanny shots. Similarly, Lindsey Davenport's opponents tried to move her away from her strength – powerful baseline hits – to force her to move in and sideways, eliminating her power.

These examples are how athletes adjust their game

to force their opponent to do something contrary to their strength. These are examples of how athletes try to control their opponents.

In other sport situations, control is more about self-control.

In baseball, a pitcher has to control his pitches. He needs good placement of his fastball and he can't let his curveball hang in the strike zone. When the pitcher has "good control," he is usually getting ahead in the count and getting batters out.

A gymnast needs good body control on the balance beam or other apparatus in order to stick the landing and remain graceful. The same goes for figure skaters.

In the spring of 1988, Temple University was totally dominating women's lacrosse. "Dominating" is a mild way to put it; they were crushing their top 10 opponents by double digits. Lafayette College went in to play them on the North Philadelphia Astroturf with a plan to control Temple's dominating power and speed. Also a strong and speedy team, Lafayette slowed the game down to a crawl, controlling the ball and looking to take only a sure shot on goal, to keep the ball out of the crosses of their dominating opponent. At halftime, the score was surprisingly close and the Lafayette players secretly dreamed they would pull off the upset.

Their strategy of control worked in the first half

but the team simple got worn out in the second half as Temple adjusted to the strategy. Temple secured the victory, remaining undefeated.

The lesson: efforts to control the other team can be temporarily effective, but are rarely sustainable.

The same is true in life. Our attempts at controlling how we want others to react or behave might work for a time, but eventually we get worn out.

Like the gymnast, our control efforts are better served when focused on ourselves.

When we can control our own behavior and our own thoughts, and, to borrow from a 12-step program, realize we are powerless over everything but ourselves, we are much more successful in all aspects of life.

That's getting ahead in the count. That's self-control.

SUZANNE DETAR

- Chapter Thirty-two -

SPORTSMANSHIP AT HOME

In the era of end zone celebrations, bench clearing brawls, and Tour de France doping, it is refreshing to witness good sportsmanship.

Having spent two days, with one more day still to go, at the Coastal Carolina Aquatics Association Championships, I learned that sportsmanship is still alive and well. Although the message on the back of the event t-shirt missed the mark by stressing individual effort over team effort and winning above good competition, the spirit of sportsmanship was on display. Swimmers, coaches and parents were complimenting their opponents' efforts as they climbed out of the pool, shaking hands across lane lines, and cheering encouragement. One unknown swimmer gave her cap to my daughter after hers broke moments before climbing on the blocks to swim.

What is good sportsmanship? According to the USA Olympic Committee materials, "An athlete who is a good sport is someone whose conduct and attitude demonstrate gracious behavior before, during, and after competition. In fact, good sportsmanship demands that nothing be done before, during, or after a game to cheapen or detract from victory."

The materials go on to give other winning examples of good sport behavior: Hugging or shaking hands with a competitor after a competition, showing appreciation for those who support you, assisting a competitor in need, acknowledging a competitor's skills to others, accepting praise with grace and humility and avoiding or deflecting all opportunities to criticize competitors or judges.

Perhaps the most poignant example of good sportsmanship I've read about was in a softball playoff game between Western Oregon and Central Washington several years ago. In a scoreless game with a regional playoff berth on the line, a Central Washington player hit a home run with two players on base. As the batter rounded first, she collapsed with a knee injury. For the home run to count, she had to round the bases, touching each one. The rules prevented her team mates from assisting her and if they put in a pinch runner, the home run would only count as a single.

In an awesome display of sportsmanship, two

opponents from Western Oregon carried her to each base. That run made the difference in the game and assured the victory for Central Washington.

These examples of sportsmanship got me to thinking about sportsmanship at home. As a parent, these examples epitomize the kind of sportsmanship I want my children to take into all aspects of their lives, not just on the field or in the pool. It's the kind of behavior that I want to display to my own family members. And, to be honest, it doesn't always happen.

Sportsmanship at home is courtesy. And courtesy isn't always easy when there are deadlines to meet, carpools to drive, lawns to mow, clothes to wash, dishes to clean, pets to walk, bills to pay, dinner to make, and on and on and on.

An unknown writer said about courtesy that it "is an expression of love, warm concern for the other person's comfort, peace of mind and well-being." The writer goes on to explain that we often overlook being courteous with the ones we love and that we miss so many opportunities to share our love in little ways.

Let's be on the lookout to carry someone around the bases, especially those who live in our homes.

SUZANNE DETAR

- Chapter Thirty-three -

AVOID OR CONFRONT

Baseball runners avoid the tag.

Quarterbacks avoid the sack.

Running backs and wide receivers avoid tacklers.

Basketball players avoid the double team.

All these athletes are successful if they avoid confrontation.

The base runner avoids confrontation with the catcher's mitt – he scores a run. The quarterback avoids confrontation with the rusher – he completes a pass. The running back or wide receiver avoids confrontation with the tacklers – he breaks free for a touchdown. The dribbler passes to avoid the double team – a basket is scored.

Avoidance in these situations seems pretty darn positive.

But, turn the situation around. The defensive players are successful if they seek confrontation. The catcher confronts the runner with the mitt – he saves a run from scoring. The rusher confronts the quarterback with his body – he drops the offense for a yard-losing sack. The tackler confronts the runner or receiver – he saves a score or breaks up a play. The double team traps the dribbler – a turnover results in a change of possession.

These defensive and offensive players confront and avoid situations seem clear, depending on your perspective, of course.

But, not all life situations have such clear delineation or obvious perspective. Deciding when to avoid or when to confront is not always easy. And deciding how to do it is even trickier.

In football, sometimes a little more subtlety in the play is required. For example, the defender rushing the quarterback can't rough the passer or have helmet to helmet contact. The lesson: confrontation must be tempered with good judgment and restraint.

Now, back to life situations. Are you an avoider or a confronter?

Personally, I tend to avoid confrontation. I'd like to extend the analogy and blame my avoidance mentality on my athletic endeavors. In sports, I was an offensive-minded player always working hard to outmanouver an opponent - dodging to avoid defenders in field hockey and shooting to avoid the goalie in lacrosse.

The sport in which I was more of a defensive player than scorer was basketball. As a defender, taking the offensive foul often hurt and, in many occasions, it was a failed attempt, stopping the play but committing the defensive foul. Worse yet was when I committed the defensive foul and the play still resulted in a score.

Properly setting up the confrontation – taking the offensive charge - required skill, courage and timing. The same is true about the pass rusher or a myriad of other athletic situations.

And the same is equally true about life situations.

Confrontation, when done properly, yields successful results. When done improperly, the negative consequences can be dramatic. On the other hand, constant avoidance of situations when confrontation is necessary also leads to negative consequences – misunderstandings, resentments and failed endeavors.

As in many situations, judgment and balance are needed. Sometimes you have to be like the aggressive defender. At other times - more like the elusive offensive player. At all times - mindful of the desired outcome, committed to playing by the rules, and respectful of the other players.

119

SUZANNE DETAR

- Chapter Thirty-four -

ASK FOR HELP

For several years our community held a "Get Fit" challenge. One year, over 300 people signed up and weighed in weekly at the recreation center. Participation at various workouts was high and community building was awesome. On top of that, the total weight loss during just the first two weeks of the program exceeded 400 pounds!

Gyms and fitness instructors offered free classes and island business offered great prizes. Our newspaper printed the percentage of weight loss and the top ten competitors on a weekly basis. The competition was tough for first place and the prize package.

But, let's face it – some of us, some of the time, may be a little too competitive for our own good. A few times during the challenge, I could put myself in that category, and, well, it hurt.

Yeah, I'm not so competitive about the weight loss thing – my percentage of loss had actually gone in the opposite direction since the challenge started, but my competitiveness came out in some of the programs. Take the Friday night "Get Fit" dodge ball event. Oh, it is so much fun to peg someone. Only problem was I hurt my shoulder by overthrowing – too hard and too many throws. But it was worth it to get one extra special competitor out at least once.

Flash forward to a Wednesday night CrossFit class. I felt the need to puke several times during that workout, which involved lots of sprints and crazy antics with a 20-pound ball. But my competitive nature wouldn't allow me to drop out of the ½ mile team run with the 20-pound ball above my head even though I pulled my butt muscle by throwing that 20-pound ball earlier in the workout to one of my partners.

So, what's a girl to do with a pulled butt muscle, a throbbing shoulder, and soreness throughout almost every muscle in her body?

Call for help. And I called on one of the Get Fit prize donors. Tara is an island resident and a massage therapist. She donated a free massage as part of the prize package and, well, she got me back in the competition.

I'd been working with Tara for several months prior to the overexertion during the "Get Fit" Challenge. Before the massage treatments started, I had such a bad shoulder that I couldn't even throw a baseball. But, deep tissue massage coupled with weight training brought that shoulder back to life…and to dodge ball. But it also gave me something else — it was a good reminder that it is okay to ask for help.

SUZANNE DETAR

- Chapter Thirty-Five -

FREE FROM FEAR

"Of all the hazards on the course, fear is the most dangerous."
- Tiger Woods, professional golfer

"The absolute worst thing a receiver can do is worry about not catching the ball or getting hit."

- Jerry Rice, professional football player

"I Aint Skerd."

- Blake Wharton, extreme sports professional MotoX driver, team "No Fear."

Woods, Rice and, yes, even Wharton in his grammatically challenged, extreme-sports-minded way, understand that fear can cripple an athlete's performance.

What golfer among us hasn't hit a barnburner straight into the water hazard immediately after fearing she would do just that?

What weekend warrior hasn't dropped a pass upon

hearing footsteps from the defender because of the dreaded fear of getting hit?

Is there a parent among us who has tried out their child's skateboard without at least the fleeting thought of falling and breaking a bone?

And in baseball there is the brush back – the pitcher pitching inside to worry a hitter – to make him fear the inside pitch.

When an athlete operates from fear, he operates from a dangerous position. His focus moves from success to defeat...making a successful play or outcome that much more difficult.

I confess to fearing the open court layup. As crazy as it might sound, when I was a high school basketball player I'd much rather shoot a layup with a defender on me as I would in the wide-open court. I just feared I was going to blow that layup. And guess what? I often did.

Fear is a mental barrier, a success inhibitor, a problem maker.

That is what Tiger Woods and Jerry Rice recognized – that much of sports competition is a mental game that requires more mental preparation than physical skill and agility.

An athlete can overcome fear by practice and by being adequately prepared, staying in good shape, seeking good coaching, and wearing protective gear.

Isn't the same true for life?

Once fear creeps into our system, we, too, operate from a dangerous position. We operate from a position that anticipates failure. When we are worried, anxious, agitated, uneasy, in a funk, panicked, distressed, dismayed, in a tizzy, all worked up, and experiencing angst long past our teen years, we have invited fear's companions into our lives. And we often create problems for ourselves where none existed.

Rice and Woods are and were known for being two of the most committed players to working hard at practice in their respective sports.

In high school, I practiced the layup over and over again until the fear was under control...and my open layup shooting percentage improved.

And although practicing away fear in other parts of our lives might not seem as simple as practicing a layup, preparation and seeking help can lead to a life that is free from the unwanted and often unwarranted fear that we let creep into our lives.

There is some relief knowing we can live by Wharton's grammatically-challenged motto, "I aint skerd."

SUZANNE DETAR

- Chapter Thirty-Six -

HARD WORK

Swimmers and parents were buzzing with excitement over the next event. Would Katie Hoff break another pool record? Hoff hopped on the blocks and clapped her hands in her trademark style.

No, this wasn't the scene from the 2008 Beijing Olympics. Hoff wasn't in The Cube. It was just a few months later and Hoff was in a 25-yard pool in an Asian community in Atlanta. And she was competing against age group swimmers from the City of Charleston Southern Marlin's Racing Team and against other USA swim clubs from the East Coast.

Just months after winning one silver and two bronze medals at the 2008 Olympics and making the morning news interview circuit, Hoff was back to the grind, practicing with her North Baltimore swim club and competing against other USA swim clubs in small pools across the country.

The stark contrast between The Cube and Atlanta's Dynamo club pool was a reminder that the spotlight of the Olympics dims quickly and that hard work in less than glamorous facilities is what leads to the big event.

- Chapter Thirty-Seven -

THE PERFECT GAME

The perfect game in baseball isn't impossible; it's just extremely rare. The last perfect game in Major League Baseball– when a pitcher gets every batter out in order without anyone ever reaching base for any reason (27 batters up and 27 batters down) - was thrown by Félix Hernández of the Seattle Mariners on August 15, 2012. And in all the years and games played in the pros, the perfect game has only been achieved 23 times. Or for statistically inclined folks, that's less than one in about every 18,000 games.

In other sports, perfection is also difficult. We may remember the amazing Olympic performances of Mary Lou Retton in 1984, who scored a perfect 10 in the floor exercise and the vault. Her perfect scores followed Nadia Comaneci's seven perfect 10s at the Montreal Olympics four years earlier.

But not one perfect 10 has been scored in a major international gymnastics' competition since 1992 and, due to a complicated scoring system, it is unlikely we will see any perfect 10s in the Olympics again.

More attainable, the perfect score in bowling is a 300, which has been achieved by many bowlers at all levels of play. To score a perfect 300 in bowling, the player must roll a strike in the first nine frames and three strikes in the last frame. More difficult and requiring more consistency, a 900 series is bowling three consecutive 300 games, which has been confirmed to have been achieved by collegiate bowler Jeremy Sonnenfeld in 1997, twice by teenager Robert Mushtare in 2005 and 2006 and by an additional 27 bowlers.

A slight imperfection in the gymnast's landing, an error by a fielder, or one pin left standing in 300, means the athlete is not perfect.

But, in many, if not most athletic endeavors, being imperfect is good enough. Most people who bowl a 299 will win the game. A team that records a "no-hitter," even if a player reaches base on an error, will most likely win the game. A gymnast who performs a routine perfectly but has a slight bobble on the landing, is still likely to win the event.

I recently learned the same goes for life as well.

Someone recently told me that I am "perfectly imperfect." The conversation was revolving around my being critical of myself – feeling inadequate after making a parenting mistake.

Having never thought of myself as a perfectionist, this conversation did get me to realize that I am self-critical when I don't do or say things perfectly and go through this internal beating up process.

I would never have associated such thoughts with being a perfectionist. But looking back on that mistake and many others for which I've lost sleep over, I can now see that I was being critical for not being perfect. And, more importantly, the outcomes of those situations turned out pretty good even if I didn't perform perfectly.

Sometimes a mistake, or something we don't do perfectly, is like pitching a no-hitter. It isn't perfect, but it's awesome. It's perfectly imperfect.

SUZANNE DETAR

ABOUT THE AUTHOR

Suzanne Detar is an award-winning writer, athlete, and newspaper publisher in Charleston, South Carolina.

Don't Lose the Ball in the Lights and Other Life Lessons from Sports is the first in Sue's Home Grown Wisdom Series. The next book in the series, *Be Goofy*, has a planned 2019 release (see excerpt starting on page 137).

Sue graduated from Temple University School of Law in 1991, where she served on the editorial staff of the Law Review.

Although she maintains her law licenses in Pennsylvania, New Jersey and South Carolina, Sue retired from the practice of law in 1997. She served as an adjunct professor of political science at Charleston

Southern University from 2002 to 2003. In 2003, she birthed a weekly newspaper on Daniel Island, SC - a developing new urban community in Charleston. Now in its 14th year, *The Daniel Island News* continues to thrive, winning many writing, photography, advertising and design awards each year.

On the sports front, Sue earned eight Division I varsity letters from Lafayette College in field hockey and lacrosse. She was instrumental in starting two successful youth sports programs in her community – a swim team and a middle school basketball program. She is currently involved in bringing field hockey to the lowcountry.

Learn more about the author, the Home Grown Wisdom Series, and other upcoming books by Sue at www.SuzanneDetar.com.

You can write to Sue at SueDetar33@gmail.com.

PLEASE WRITE A REVIEW

Thank you for reading this book. If you enjoyed the book, or have other feedback that would be valuable to readers or which provides constructive ideas for improving this book or the Home Grown Wisdom series, please go to any online distributor of this book and write an engaging and constructive review.

Excerpts from *Be Goofy*, Sue's next book in the Home Grown Wisdom Series

Sample Chapter - Be Goofy

Be goofy. It's fun. It's liberating. And, most importantly, it encourages you to be yourself.

Right now, "Be Goofy" is posted in large letters on my fridge.

I looked "goofy" up in the dictionary. It means "silly."

The older I get, the less I worry about how goofy or silly I am. Think about the Disney character Goofy. We love him, and he is goofy as all get out! We admire his good heart and his self-confidence to be who he is. Yes, self-confidence. While it appears that Goofy is clueless about his goofiness, I think it's the opposite of cluelessness. He is content to be the goofy dog that he is. His creator, Art Babbitt, described him as "a composite of an everlasting optimist" and as "a gullible Good Samaritan." That is silly in the most marvelous way!

Being goofy is about giving yourself permission to be yourself. Being goofy is not worrying about what other people think. Being goofy is about letting go. And, it's about being an optimist and a Good Samaritan.

Here is a strange - and goofy - confession. Sometimes I stand in front of the mirror and make really, really goofy faces. Oddly enough, it always makes me feel good and I always end up laughing! Perhaps it's my way of not taking myself too seriously. I encourage you to give it a try!

My kids, when they were in their early teens, used to get extremely embarrassed by how nerdy and goofy I could be. Back then, I danced badly and frequently. And sometimes I did it in public and in their presence. While they thought it was goofy then, now they remember it fondly.

The truth is – I don't need the reminder on my fridge. I come by my goofiness naturally! It's really there as a reminder to be myself.

Now, all this said, maybe goofiness isn't your thing. What is? Figure it out and do it. Be yourself.

DON'T LOSE THE BALL IN THE LIGHTS